PARADE
OF THE
PIPERS

T0328019

Written by Richard O'Neill and Michelle Russell

Illustrated by Elijah Vardo

Collins

CHAPTER 1

There was once a town, a very busy town, with a large factory built of red sandstone.

The factory was owned and run by one all-ruling, all-seeing giant. Although no one had ever seen the Giant, the townsfolk *knew* it had to be a giant because a ginormous house towered over the town and that was where the Giant lived. So, as you have yet to meet the illusive occupant of the opulent house that sits grandly above the town, we'll simply call them the Giant.

The Giant owned the houses and the shops too. Even the tiny park, at the far edge of the town, was owned by the Giant.

Everything about the town was busy. The townsfolk were always rushing here and there. That was the pace the Giant wanted, and who were they to disagree?

Things had to be done immediately, as if everything was an emergency. And once that thing was done, there was yet another thing to do. It was like everyone had a neverending "to-do list" that went on and on and on.

The lights burnt all night, which pleased the Giant, as the night-burning lights meant that the town could run as if it was daytime. As such, it was hard to tell when day ended and when night began.

The people worked hard to make the things that the factory churned out. The wages were good, but the people, being tired and bored of doing the same thing every day, bought things to cheer themselves up.

Each week at the factory was similar to the previous one. Day after day, the townsfolk yearned to buy the next best thing that was better than the thing they'd bought the week before. At the end of every week, they were ready to spend everything they had, before once again returning to the factory to begin the whole cycle again.

5

While the adults in the town spent their time going to work to make their money and then going shopping to spend their hard-earned cash, the children of the town spent less and less time with the adults.

In the morning, the adults were like busy bees, always rushing to work, and by the evenings, they were all too tired to do anything but rest. The adults and children had less time to talk to each other and the games they once played were a distant memory.

The laughter and giggles that once flowed freely from the children slowly disappeared.

New!

Latest model!

New!

Don't miss out!

Buy now!

With an abundance of new things, the people in the town rarely looked after the things they already had. If the novelty wore off or the new thing broke, which often happened, it was thrown away and replaced with the latest model. Surrounded by so many gizmos and gadgets, there was little time to care about what happened to the old items.

Everyone knew that things were just not meant to last. But not to worry, they also knew that the Giant's council would be endorsing the newest version just in time for a model relaunch.

This explained the huge piles of junk that were slowly turning into ginormous mounds of junk on the outside of the town, next to the mountains and the stream. No one really cared, because they never had the time to enjoy or even notice the surrounding countryside.

They only began to notice the amount of junk around the town when it started to become a problem.
But even then, they didn't seem to have time to sort it out, so they simply manoeuvred around it, as best they could.

The junk piled up throughout the town, and soon every street and avenue had a junk pile tower.

When the Giant eventually investigated the cause of some people arriving late for work, they discovered the grumbling and cries of the people, as they dodged the tumbling debris.

This was a problem, a huge and growing one, and questions were asked: How did this happen? What could be done? Could it be sorted out quickly? But who could be called upon to fix the problem?

Why us, of course!

And that is why the Giant got in touch with us – our reputation of making things *clean as a whistle* – so we, the Pipers, were invited to the town. We accepted the invitation on one condition – that we could celebrate with a parade. Determined to get the town tidied up, but doubtful that there would be time for any kind of celebration, the Giant reluctantly agreed to our terms.

Everyone was so focused on their work that they nearly missed the Giant's announcement that the Travelling Pipers would be visiting. With all the detours to bypass the junk towers, it was taking them longer to travel to and from work – would they even have time to watch a parade?

CHAPTER 2

The Giant called us the Pipers, but that's only one of the things we do. We mainly pipe for fun, along with storytelling and dancing, but our real work is recycling and cleaning, as we travel from place to place, living in our caravans. These are pulled by a variety of vehicles, all of which are built or rebuilt by ourselves, from used parts and whole vehicles, even salvaging the parts that have been left to rot. Some would say we're like magicians, able to make something out of nothing.

Camping on the edge of the town, venturing a little
bit further off our travelling route, intrigued by
the Giant's plea, we chatted about the new place and
the opportunities it might hold. Their trash could be
our treasure. Their story, a tale to be shared and told.

The next day, some of us went
into the town, following the map
the Giant had sent.

Avoiding the towers of wobbling
junk, we soon realised that this was
why our help was needed. Instead of
meeting the Giant, we were
presented with a large envelope;
inside, a note explained that
the Giant was too busy to meet us,
followed by a long list of instructions
and rules about what we could and
could not do.

In no time at all, we got to work,
cleaning and tidying, making
the gardens around the Giant's
mansion look perfectly neat.

As well as getting paid to take away
all the rubbish, we were able to
recycle it, which was like getting paid
twice – a delightful bonus, if you will.

As we got closer to the smaller buildings in the town, which looked extra small beside the wavering towers of junk, we noticed that despite the endless whirring and hissing and thumping of some of the factory machines, with an occasional thunder-crack, the people didn't seem to notice the noise.

We also noticed that there was no music to be heard anywhere! It was believed that the Giant found it distracting, or rather he thought it would be distracting for the workers. So, when we stopped for a cup of tea, my old uncle got his little set of pipes out, the ones he'd made from thrown-away water tubes, and we made some music to keep us going into the afternoon.

Clang clang clunk cling, cried our metal shovels.

Swoosh swoosh swash swish, swished our sweeping brush.

Screep scratch scrape, went the wide-pronged rake.

Feeling the urge to dance, as our tools transformed the air into an orchestral symphony, we shared our rhymes.

Now you know the reason why some other Travellers call us the Rhyme Steppers.

As we tapped out a beat, the music flowed, weaving a hypnotic tune through the streets. The melody entered the open windows and doors, which caught the attention of the townsfolk. One by one, the people began to slow down and stopped what they were doing. They were mesmerised by the sounds they heard.

Then something happened that had never happened before.

Distracted by the music, the production line that had never ever stopped came to a grinding halt!

This was not good news for the Giant, who was beginning to regret sending the invitation to us Pipers.

As the music played, another sound could be heard. A sound that had been there before but had been drowned out by the whirring and whizzing of the machines in the factory. A *creak* and a *crack* could be heard as the piles of junk swayed. A sound that once was not noticed was now gaining the attention of the townsfolk, and they began really to notice how much junk was piled up.

Again, this was not good news for the Giant!

21

CHAPTER 3

Annoyed, the Giant sent a message that the people had better get back to work or else there would be no parade, and if there was any more singing and dancing while they cleared the junk, us Pipers wouldn't get paid!

Having been so busy, some people had missed the first announcement about the parade. Now that everyone had stopped working and they began to learn of it, they started to look forward to the singing and dancing that would take place.

Although one of the Pipers' missions is to demonstrate how music and movement go together beautifully to make work fun, we adhered to the Giant's order.

The cogs of the machines started turning again, but now that the people were aware of the creaks and groans of the junk piles wavering, they took more notice of it as they dashed here, there and everywhere. They also noticed the Travellers carefully dismantling and sorting the different pieces that once had looked like a giant 3D jigsaw puzzle.

As the Travellers took away more pieces, the height of the piles reduced in size and the creaking and cracking sounds became quieter.

Although the sounds of the factory could still be heard, it became more like a hum, and the people began to tune into the tweets and calls of the birds who were celebrating their tree tops becoming clear. Lower down to the ground, the bees could be heard buzzing as they busied themselves collecting nectar from the few flowers that had survived in the shadows of the junk piles – now proudly blooming and swaying in the summer breeze that seemed to move more easily through the town.

The factory continued to work at top speed, but outside the factory, the pace of the people began to slow down. They became more interested in what us Travellers were doing. Some of them even began to help us on their short tea and lunch breaks. Although we couldn't sing or dance, there was no rule saying we couldn't chat while we worked.

As we chatted with the people and told them all about our way of life, the piles of junk began to reduce in size and the town began to look neat and clean once more. A team effort all round deserved a nice cup of tea, which was kindly shared by the people who lived nearby.

While some of the people looked on, puzzled and worried, and others continued to ignore us, some became more curious about what was happening to the junk and wondered why something that was once useless, discarded and thrown away was being treated with care. Happy to answer the questions put to us, we explained why we valued the junk and the marvellous things that it could become as it was reused, recycled and upcycled.

Inspired to have a go themselves, we began to show the townsfolk how to use the tools, which for some was very tricky as they were so used to working at the fastest possible pace set by the Giant and the machines.

We shared a rhyme, and we chanted as we
taught them:

"More haste less speed, gets the job done,

More haste less speed, with ease brings the fun."

They beamed as they enjoyed using their own hands
to find pieces of junk, which were slowly put together
to make new and exciting things.

When it was time to return to the factory, the townsfolk didn't want to go back. They didn't say anything, they just looked at each other and gave us a smile.

We Travellers, already knowing the benefits of being outdoors and looking after the world around us, smiled back as we witnessed the transformation of the townsfolk.

The people were happy
now that they were making
a difference to their town,
but some of them began to
wonder what impact this
would have, and then began
to worry about what the Giant
might do about it.

It wouldn't take long for
the Giant to notice that
the factory was now at
a standstill and stood empty.
What would the Giant do?
Whatever it was, it couldn't
be as bad as what they had
being putting up with over
the years, missing out on time
with their family and friends.

It was a funny feeling –
a mixture of excitement
and doubt, happiness
and sadness.

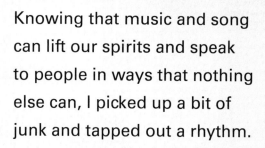

Knowing that music and song
can lift our spirits and speak
to people in ways that nothing
else can, I picked up a bit of
junk and tapped out a rhythm.

This was replicated by
a fellow Traveller, and soon by
all the Travellers and townsfolk.
The rhythm rippled throughout
the town. The melodies came
soon after the rhythm, followed
by the words. Rhythm, melody,
words and voices – soon there
was a song about a giant and
a factory and the need to spend
more time with family.

But not working would
mean no money, which was
important for buying the food
they needed. So, reluctantly,
the townsfolk returned to
the factory.

While us Travellers continued to collect and sort
the junk, the song continued to play in the minds of
the people. While they were working in the factory,
from time to time, a reminder of the song could
be heard as the workers hummed or whistled
the familiar tune.

It was a tune that followed them home, which was shared with their families and lulled young babies as they drifted off to sleep. Some say they even dreamt about the song while they slept.

The song now sung at the breakfast table seemed to give an extra spring in the step of the townsfolk as they left their homes for work.

During their breaks, the townsfolk joined us, the rhythm and rhyme connecting us even more to the nature that surrounded us – the birds and the bees adding their own unique sounds while the breeze trickled by, the tree tops whistling and the flower buds swaying.

Together, Travellers and townsfolk worked in
harmony and the junk became a distant memory as
it disappeared from sight, changing the town in more
ways than could ever have been imagined.

CHAPTER 4

The music that was giving people confidence, note by note, was also beginning to lift the sadness that had loomed over the town.

One by one, smiles and laughter began to return to the children.

A forgotten, yet familiar sound to the Giant's ears, the giggling became contagious and made the Giant do something that he had never done before.

The elaborate doorknob of the Giant's house turned clockwise and as it did so, the *clunk* and *click* of a key unlocked the door. The sound resonated around the town and made everyone stop and look. A heaviness began to weigh down as everyone's eyes were fixed on the large door, which began to creak open to reveal a gigantic shadow. Holding their breath, the townsfolk prepared themselves for the consequences of breaking the Giant's rule of merriment.

All of the townsfolk and Travellers were transfixed by the shadow that became more of a haze. Then a small figure slowly stepped forward and waved to the onlookers who gradually began to realise that the Giant was not a giant at all, just an average-sized adult.

While we stood there speechless, a small, barely audible voice could be heard. The not-so-giant person had taken a deep breath to cautiously introduce himself as Cosmos.

Stunned by the Giant's appearance, our heads began to burst with so many questions, while our ability to speak seemed to be lost or frozen.

The silence was finally broken as a small girl stepped forward. The kindness of her smile was soon reflected in the faces of everyone nearby, including Cosmos.

A warm, friendly welcome sparked a renewed confidence in Cosmos, who happily answered our endless questions.

A sad story unfolded, as we discovered that when Cosmos was young, he'd wanted to become a musician, but his dreams were shattered when he was told that any thoughts of music making were a waste of valuable working time.

Hearing the transformation that the music and dance had brought to the townsfolk, Cosmos began to realise that what he'd been told and always believed was wrong. This filled him with a confidence that

he thought had long been lost, and he accepted the little girl's invitation to join the parade without any hesitation. No one was more surprised than Cosmos when his loud announcement bellowed at the start of the parade.

Together, Cosmos and the townsfolk, every adult and child, followed the Travellers as they snaked their way through the town. The creaks and cracks were now just a distant memory.

Before the Travellers were drawn to the "call of the road", we gifted Cosmos some instruments that had been recycled from the junk. We promised to return to the town the following year for what would be another magnificent parade to celebrate the teamwork that would go into keeping the town clean and tidy.

THE PIPERS' SONG

Once in a land not
so far away,
people worked hard
through the night and day.

Sadness loomed
all around the town,
laughter lost
replaced with a frown.

To cheer themselves up,
a new thing to buy,
the junk that piled up
would make you cry.

Until ...

The Giant called out
to a marvellous troop,
with a swish and a swoosh,
a sweep and a swoop.

More haste less speed,
gets the job done,
more haste less speed,
with ease brings the fun.

As the smiles
and the merriment reappeared,
the fear and the junk
all disappeared.

The Giant felt brave
and opened their door,
opened their heart,
revealed so much more.

Not a giant at all,
it was all a charade,
freedom now found
in the Pipers' Parade.

✿ Ideas for reading ✿

Written by Gill Matthews
Primary Literacy Consultant

Reading objectives:
- check that the text makes sense to them, discuss their understanding, and explaining the meaning of words in context
- ask questions to improve their understanding of a text
- draw inferences such as inferring characters' feelings, thoughts and motives from their actions, and justifying inferences with evidence

Spoken language objectives:
- use relevant strategies to build their vocabulary
- articulate and justify answers, arguments and opinions
- participate in discussions, presentations, performances, role play, improvisations and debates

Curriculum links: Art and Design

Interest words: elaborate, resonated, transfixed

Build a context for reading
- Ask children to look closely at the front cover and to read the title. Explore what the title means to them.
- Read the back-cover blurb. Ask questions that explore children's understanding of the blurb e.g. What do you think *Travelling recyclers* are? What impact do you think their work might have? Discuss with children the capital letter on *Travelling*, and ask them why they think it has been used.
- Ask children what characters they expect to read about in the story.

Understand and apply reading strategies
- Read pp2–5 aloud, using meaning and punctuation to help you read with appropriate expression. Ask children what they have found out about the town and the people who live there.
- Return to p2 and explore some of the vocabulary. Ask children how they think the Giant can be *all-ruling* and *all-seeing*.
- Children can read pp6–13. Ask them how they think it must feel to live in the town. How do they think the Travelling Pipers might help the town and the townsfolk?
- Give children the opportunity to read the rest of the story.